GEARING UP FOR SPORTS!

FOOTBALL GEAR

NOAH RICCARDI

PowerKiDS press

Published in 2027 by The Rosen Publishing Group, Inc.
2544 Clinton Street, Buffalo, NY 14224

First Edition

Book Design: Madison Thogmartin

Photo Credits: Cover, p. 1 JoeSAPhotos/Shutterstock.com; p. 5 Grindstone Media Group/Shutterstock.com; p. 7 dotshock/Shutterstock.com; p. 9 Jamie Lamor Thompson/Shutterstock.com; p. 11 Everett Collection/Shutterstock.com; p. 13 Brocreative/Shutterstock.com; p. 15 Richard Paul Kane/Shutterstock.com; p. 17 Dario Zg/Shutterstock.com; p. 19 Jerry Sharp/Shutterstock.com; p. 21 Bob Cullinan/Shutterstock.com.

Cataloging-in-Publication Data
Names: Riccardi, Noah.
Title: Football gear / Noah Riccardi.
Description: Buffalo, New York : PowerKids Press, 2027. | Series: Gearing up for sports! | Includes glossary and index.
Identifiers: ISBN 9781499456677 (pbk.) | ISBN 9781499456684 (library bound) | ISBN 9781499456691 (ebook)
Subjects: LCSH: Football--Juvenile literature. | Football--Equipment and supplies--Juvenile literature.
Classification: LCC GV950.7 R533 2027 | DDC 796.332--dc23

Manufactured in China

CPSIA Compliance Information: Batch #QS27PK. For Further Information contact Rosen Publishing, at 1-800-237-9932.

CONTENTS

The Ball

Football players move a ball down the field. The ball is shaped like an egg with pointy ends. Its **surface** is **leather** and bumpy. There are laces on one side.

The laces help players throw the ball. Players put their fingers on the laces as they throw. This makes the ball **spiral** in the air. As a result, it flies further than if it didn't spin.

The Helmet

Football players often tackle and **collide** with one another. So, they wear lots of **protective** gear. Helmets help their heads. A helmet has a hard outer shell. There is soft padding inside.

ACC
Riddell

The first football helmets were simple leather caps. In the 1930s and 1940s, players started using hard plastic helmets. These **evolved** into today's helmets.

Shoulder Pads

Shoulder pads are also protective gear. Players wear them to stay safe during tackles. Shoulder pads cover and protect the upper body. The pads help players make tackles without getting hurt.

Even with pads, players can still get hurt. This is why **technique** is important. Coaches can show players good technique. This can help players learn ways to play safely.

ACC
11
41

Shoes

Football players wear shoes with spikes on the bottom. These shoes are called cleats. They help players run on grass. Football cleats have high sides. These hold the player's ankles steady. They help prevent **injury**.

DRAGONS
PATRIOTS

Kickers sometimes wear special cleats when they are playing. Kickers' cleats are lighter and similar to soccer cleats. This helps them kick the ball more accurately. Some players only wear the kicking cleat on their kicking foot.

Flag Football

In flag football, players try to grab a flag from an opponent's belt. Each player wears several flags on their belt. The play ends when the player with the ball has their flag pulled. There is no tackling.

NAIA
NIRSA
FLAG
72
adidas

GLOSSARY

collide: To run into.

evolved: Changed slowly over time.

injury: When a player gets hurt during a game.

leather: A material made from an animal's skin.

protective: Made to prevent harm.

spiral: To spin through the air.

surface: The outside layer of something.

technique: A way of doing something that requires skill.

FOR MORE INFORMATION

BOOKS

Flynn, Brendan. *Football*. Minneapolis, MN: Abdo Publishing, 2024.

Leed, Percy. *Football Superstars*. Minneapolis, MN: Lerner Publications, 2025.

WEBSITES

NFL: Play Football
playfootball.nfl.com/
Learn how to get started playing football.

Olympics: Flag Football
olympics.com/en/sports/flag-football/
Flag football will be part of the Olympic Games in 2028!

INDEX